EMMANUEL JOSEPH

China's Legal Frontier, The Rise of a Superpower in the ICC

Copyright © 2025 by Emmanuel Joseph

All rights reserved. No part of this publication may be reproduced, stored or transmitted in any form or by any means, electronic, mechanical, photocopying, recording, scanning, or otherwise without written permission from the publisher. It is illegal to copy this book, post it to a website, or distribute it by any other means without permission.

First edition

This book was professionally typeset on Reedsy.
Find out more at reedsy.com

Contents

1 Chapter 1: The Birth of the International Criminal Court... 1
2 Chapter 2: China's Legal Evolution 3
3 Chapter 3: China's Decision on the Rome Statute 5
4 Chapter 4: The Sovereignty Dilemma 7
5 Chapter 5: Diplomatic Maneuvering 9
6 Chapter 6: China's Influence in International Organizations 11
7 Chapter 7: The Human Rights Debate 13
8 Chapter 8: Legal Aspects of the Belt and Road Initiative 15
9 Chapter 9: Prospects for Future Engagement 17
10 Chapter 10: Comparative Perspectives 19
11 Chapter 11: Scholarly Perspectives 21
12 Chapter 12: Conclusion and Reflection 23

1

Chapter 1: The Birth of the International Criminal Court (ICC)

The establishment of the International Criminal Court (ICC) marked a significant milestone in the pursuit of global justice. Founded on July 1, 2002, through the Rome Statute, the ICC was created to prosecute individuals for the most severe international crimes: genocide, war crimes, and crimes against humanity. The court's creation was the culmination of decades of negotiations and advocacy by states and non-governmental organizations. The idea of an international court dates back to the aftermath of World War II, but it took nearly six decades for the international community to agree on a permanent institution. The ICC's headquarters in The Hague symbolizes its mission to uphold the rule of law across borders, providing a forum for justice where national systems fail.

The ICC operates based on the principle of complementarity, meaning it only intervenes when national jurisdictions are unable or unwilling to prosecute alleged criminals. This principle is crucial in maintaining the sovereignty of states while ensuring that perpetrators of heinous crimes do not escape justice. The court's jurisdiction is limited to crimes committed after its establishment and is restricted to cases involving individuals from member states or crimes committed on their territories. Despite these limitations, the ICC has made significant strides in holding accountable those responsible for grave violations of human rights.

One of the ICC's landmark cases was the prosecution of Thomas Lubanga Dyilo, a Congolese warlord convicted of conscripting child soldiers. This case highlighted the court's commitment to protecting vulnerable populations and established precedents for future prosecutions. However, the ICC has also faced challenges, including accusations of bias, limited enforcement mechanisms, and political interference. Critics argue that the court disproportionately targets African states, leading to allegations of neo-colonialism and undermining its legitimacy.

The ICC's success relies heavily on the cooperation of its member states, as the court lacks its own enforcement arm. States are responsible for arresting and surrendering suspects, which can be problematic when dealing with powerful individuals or countries that refuse to comply. Additionally, the court's reliance on voluntary contributions and the lack of universal membership pose significant financial and operational challenges. Despite these obstacles, the ICC remains a beacon of hope for victims of atrocities, striving to bring justice to the world's most vulnerable.

2

Chapter 2: China's Legal Evolution

China's legal system has undergone a profound transformation over the past few decades, reflecting the country's rapid economic growth and increasing engagement with the international community. Historically, China was skeptical of international law, viewing it as a tool of Western dominance. However, as China's global influence has grown, so has its participation in international legal frameworks. This chapter explores China's legal evolution, from its early isolationist policies to its current position as a major player in global governance.

In the early years of the People's Republic of China, the country prioritized sovereignty and non-interference in its domestic affairs. This stance was rooted in China's colonial history and the belief that international law was biased against non-Western nations. However, China's economic reforms in the late 20th century ushered in a new era of engagement with the world. The country began to participate in international organizations and treaties, gradually integrating international legal norms into its domestic legal system.

China's accession to the World Trade Organization (WTO) in 2001 marked a significant turning point in its legal development. The WTO membership required China to undertake extensive legal reforms, aligning its trade policies with international standards. These reforms had a ripple effect on other areas of Chinese law, leading to greater transparency, predictability, and rule of law. China's growing legal sophistication is evident in its active participation in international arbitration and dispute resolution mechanisms.

Despite these advancements, China's approach to international law remains cautious and pragmatic. The country often emphasizes the importance of state sovereignty and the need for a balanced and fair international legal order. China has been selective in its adoption of international legal norms, prioritizing those that align with its national interests. This cautious approach is reflected in China's relationship with the ICC, where the country has taken a measured stance, weighing the benefits and risks of deeper engagement.

3

Chapter 3: China's Decision on the Rome Statute

The Rome Statute, adopted in 1998, serves as the foundational treaty of the ICC. It outlines the court's jurisdiction, functions, and structure, providing a legal framework for prosecuting international crimes. China participated in the negotiations leading to the Rome Statute but ultimately decided not to ratify it. This chapter delves into the reasons behind China's decision, examining the domestic and international factors that influenced its stance.

China's primary concern with the Rome Statute was its perceived infringement on state sovereignty. The statute grants the ICC the authority to prosecute individuals without the consent of their home countries, a provision that China viewed as a potential threat to its national sovereignty. Additionally, the principle of complementarity, while aimed at respecting national jurisdictions, raised concerns about the ICC's ability to intervene in domestic legal matters.

Another key factor in China's decision was the potential for political misuse of the ICC. China feared that the court could be used as a tool for political manipulation, targeting specific countries or individuals for strategic reasons. This concern was heightened by the experiences of other countries facing ICC investigations, which sometimes appeared to be influenced by geopolitical considerations. China's leadership was wary of exposing itself to similar vulnerabilities.

Domestic legal principles also played a significant role in China's decision. The Chinese legal system, with its unique blend of civil law and socialist legal traditions, differs significantly from the common law systems prevalent in many ICC member states. China's leaders were concerned that the ICC's procedures and legal standards might not be compatible with the Chinese legal framework. This concern extended to issues such as the admissibility of evidence, the rights of defendants, and the overall fairness of ICC trials.

Ultimately, China's decision not to ratify the Rome Statute reflects a balance of pragmatism and caution. While the country acknowledges the importance of international justice, it prioritizes the protection of its sovereignty and the integrity of its legal system. As China's global influence continues to grow, its relationship with the ICC remains a subject of interest and speculation, with potential implications for the future of international criminal justice.

4

Chapter 4: The Sovereignty Dilemma

The tension between national sovereignty and international justice lies at the heart of China's objections to the ICC. Sovereignty is a core principle of the Chinese state, deeply rooted in its history and political philosophy. This chapter explores the sovereignty dilemma, analyzing China's legal and political arguments against the ICC's potential interventions in domestic affairs.

Sovereignty, as understood by China, encompasses the right to self-determination, territorial integrity, and non-interference in internal matters. This principle has been a cornerstone of Chinese foreign policy, shaped by the country's experiences with colonialism and foreign intervention. China's leadership views the protection of sovereignty as essential to maintaining stability and national unity, particularly in regions with complex political dynamics such as Tibet, Xinjiang, and Hong Kong.

China's objections to the ICC often revolve around the court's perceived encroachment on state sovereignty. The Rome Statute grants the ICC the authority to prosecute individuals even if their home countries are unwilling or unable to do so. China argues that this provision undermines the sovereignty of states, allowing external actors to interfere in domestic legal matters. Beijing is particularly concerned about the potential for politically motivated prosecutions targeting its leaders or officials.

The principle of complementarity, while intended to respect national jurisdictions, also raises concerns for China. The ICC intervenes only when national courts are unable or unwilling to prosecute alleged criminals. However, China's legal system differs significantly from those of many ICC member states, leading to questions about the compatibility of legal standards and procedures. China's leaders are wary of the ICC's potential to challenge the legitimacy of their domestic legal processes.

China's stance on sovereignty and international justice is further complicated by its role as a major global power. As China expands its influence through initiatives like the Belt and Road, it faces increasing scrutiny and calls for accountability. The sovereignty dilemma becomes more pronounced as China navigates the balance between upholding its national interests and engaging with international legal norms. This chapter delves into the complexities of this dilemma, highlighting the broader implications for global governance.

5

Chapter 5: Diplomatic Maneuvering

China's approach to the ICC is characterized by strategic diplomatic maneuvering. The country has actively engaged in international legal and diplomatic forums to shape global norms and protect its interests. This chapter examines China's diplomatic strategies, focusing on key instances where China has influenced ICC-related matters and international criminal justice.

One notable example of China's diplomatic maneuvering is its role in the United Nations Security Council (UNSC). As a permanent member with veto power, China has the ability to influence decisions related to ICC referrals and interventions. China has used this position to advocate for its principles of non-interference and state sovereignty. For instance, China has blocked or abstained from resolutions referring situations in countries like Syria and Sudan to the ICC, citing concerns about political bias and the potential for exacerbating conflicts.

China has also leveraged its economic and political influence to build alliances with other states that share its views on sovereignty and non-interference. Through initiatives like the Belt and Road and regional organizations like the Shanghai Cooperation Organization, China has fostered cooperation with countries that are skeptical of the ICC's interventions. This network of alliances strengthens China's position in international legal debates and allows it to promote alternative models of international justice.

In addition to its diplomatic efforts, China has invested in developing its own legal capacities to address international crimes. The country has established specialized courts and legal frameworks to prosecute individuals accused of serious crimes, demonstrating its commitment to justice while maintaining control over its legal processes. By enhancing its domestic legal capabilities, China aims to reduce the perceived need for external interventions and reinforce its sovereignty.

China's diplomatic maneuvering is not limited to blocking ICC actions; it also involves constructive engagement. China has participated constructively in international legal forums, contributing to discussions on reforms and improvements to the ICC. By engaging in these dialogues, China seeks to influence the direction of international criminal justice in ways that align with its principles. This dual approach of blocking unfavorable actions while participating in constructive discourse demonstrates China's nuanced and multifaceted strategy.

China's diplomatic maneuvering extends to its participation in the drafting and negotiation of international treaties. The country has been involved in shaping the legal frameworks that govern international criminal justice, advocating for provisions that respect state sovereignty and the principle of non-interference. Through these efforts, China aims to create a more balanced and equitable international legal order that accommodates diverse legal traditions and perspectives.

Furthermore, China has hosted international conferences and forums to promote dialogue on issues related to international criminal justice. These events provide platforms for states, legal experts, and scholars to exchange ideas and build consensus on key legal principles. By facilitating these discussions, China positions itself as a leader in the global legal community and reinforces its commitment to constructive engagement.

Overall, China's diplomatic maneuvering reflects a strategic blend of assertiveness and cooperation. The country seeks to protect its national interests while contributing to the development of international legal norms. China's approach to the ICC is a testament to its evolving role in global governance and its efforts to balance sovereignty with international justice.

6

Chapter 6: China's Influence in International Organizations

China's growing influence in international organizations has had significant implications for the global legal landscape. As China has risen to prominence as a global power, it has sought to shape the norms and standards that govern international relations. This chapter examines China's strategic engagement with various international organizations and its impact on international criminal justice.

China's participation in the United Nations (UN) is a key aspect of its global influence. As a permanent member of the Security Council, China plays a crucial role in shaping decisions related to international peace and security. China's veto power allows it to block resolutions that it perceives as contrary to its interests, including those related to ICC interventions. Through its active engagement in the UN, China seeks to promote principles of non-interference and respect for sovereignty.

In addition to the UN, China has been actively involved in the World Trade Organization (WTO) and other economic forums. China's integration into the global economy has necessitated legal reforms and greater adherence to international standards. This engagement has also provided China with platforms to advocate for its legal principles and challenge existing norms that it views as biased. China's influence in economic organizations extends to issues of international criminal justice, as economic stability and rule of law are interconnected.

China's participation in regional organizations, such as the Shanghai Cooperation Organization (SCO) and the Asia-Pacific Economic Cooperation (APEC), further demonstrates its strategic approach to international engagement. These organizations provide platforms for China to collaborate with neighboring countries and promote regional stability. Through these alliances, China seeks to foster a cooperative approach to international criminal justice that respects regional diversity and legal traditions.

China's influence is also evident in its leadership of initiatives such as the Belt and Road. The BRI has legal dimensions, including dispute resolution mechanisms and international arbitration. China's efforts to establish legal frameworks for the BRI reflect its desire to create a predictable and stable environment for international investment. These initiatives also provide opportunities for China to shape the legal norms governing international trade and investment.

Overall, China's engagement with international organizations highlights its commitment to shaping the global legal order. By actively participating in these forums, China aims to promote legal principles that align with its interests and contribute to a more balanced and equitable system of international criminal justice.

7

Chapter 7: The Human Rights Debate

China's human rights record has been a subject of international scrutiny and debate. The ICC's mandate to address human rights violations adds another layer of complexity to China's relationship with the court. This chapter explores the interplay between China's human rights policies and its stance on the ICC, examining the criticisms and responses from both sides.

China's human rights policies are shaped by its unique political and cultural context. The Chinese government prioritizes economic development and social stability, often viewing these goals as prerequisites for the realization of human rights. This approach contrasts with the Western emphasis on individual civil and political rights. China argues that its policies have lifted millions out of poverty and improved the overall well-being of its population.

Critics, however, argue that China's human rights record is marred by significant violations, including restrictions on freedom of speech, assembly, and religion. Issues such as the treatment of ethnic minorities in Xinjiang, the situation in Tibet, and the crackdown on political dissent have drawn international condemnation. Human rights organizations and foreign governments have called for greater accountability and transparency in China's human rights practices.

China's response to these criticisms often involves emphasizing the principle of non-interference in domestic affairs. The Chinese government argues that human rights should be considered within the context of each country's specific conditions and development stage. China contends that external pressure and interventions are counterproductive and can exacerbate internal tensions.

The ICC's involvement in human rights issues adds another layer of complexity to this debate. China's concerns about sovereignty and political misuse of the ICC are heightened when it comes to human rights. The Chinese government fears that the court could be used to target its leaders and officials for political reasons, undermining its efforts to maintain stability and development.

Despite these tensions, there are areas of potential cooperation between China and the ICC on human rights issues. China has expressed support for international efforts to combat crimes such as human trafficking, terrorism, and drug trafficking. These areas of common interest provide opportunities for dialogue and collaboration, even as differences persist on other aspects of human rights.

8

Chapter 8: Legal Aspects of the Belt and Road Initiative

The Belt and Road Initiative (BRI) is one of China's most ambitious and far-reaching projects, with significant implications for international law and governance. This chapter analyzes the legal dimensions of the BRI, including the establishment of dispute resolution mechanisms, the role of international arbitration, and the impact on China's relationship with the ICC.

The BRI involves extensive infrastructure projects and investments across Asia, Africa, and Europe. These projects require robust legal frameworks to address potential disputes and ensure the smooth implementation of agreements. China has taken steps to develop legal mechanisms that provide a predictable and stable environment for BRI investments. These mechanisms include bilateral and multilateral agreements, as well as the establishment of specialized courts and arbitration centers.

International arbitration plays a crucial role in resolving disputes related to the BRI. China has actively participated in international arbitration institutions and has promoted the use of arbitration clauses in BRI contracts. By engaging in international arbitration, China aims to build confidence among foreign investors and ensure that disputes are resolved in a fair and transparent manner. This approach aligns with China's broader goal of enhancing its legal capabilities and integrating with global legal standards.

The legal aspects of the BRI also intersect with issues of international criminal justice. As China expands its economic influence through the BRI, it faces increased scrutiny and calls for accountability. The ICC's mandate to address crimes such as corruption and economic crimes adds a layer of complexity to China's legal engagements. China must navigate the balance between promoting economic development and ensuring compliance with international legal norms.

The BRI also provides opportunities for legal cooperation and capacity building. China has offered legal training and support to BRI partner countries, helping them develop their legal systems and improve their adherence to international standards. This cooperation enhances the legal infrastructure of BRI countries and promotes a more stable and predictable legal environment for international trade and investment.

In conclusion, the legal dimensions of the BRI highlight China's commitment to creating a stable and predictable legal framework for its global initiatives. By engaging in international arbitration and developing robust legal mechanisms, China aims to build confidence among investors and promote the success of the BRI. This approach also underscores the interconnectedness of economic development and international criminal justice in China's legal strategy.

9

Chapter 9: Prospects for Future Engagement

As China's global influence continues to grow, the question of its future engagement with the ICC remains a topic of interest and speculation. This chapter explores the potential scenarios in which China might reconsider its stance on the ICC, the factors that could lead to a shift in policy, and the possible consequences for international justice and global governance.

One potential scenario for China's future engagement with the ICC involves a gradual shift in its approach to international criminal justice. As China becomes more integrated into the global legal system and gains greater confidence in its legal capabilities, it may be more willing to engage with the ICC. This shift could be driven by a recognition of the benefits of participating in a global institution dedicated to upholding justice and the rule of law.

Domestic factors could also influence China's future engagement with the ICC. As China's legal system continues to evolve and reform, there may be greater alignment with international legal standards. This alignment could reduce the perceived incompatibility between China's domestic legal principles and the ICC's procedures. Additionally, increased public awareness and demand for accountability could push the Chinese government to reconsider its stance on the ICC.

International pressure and diplomatic considerations could play a role in shaping China's future engagement with the ICC. As China seeks to enhance its global reputation and leadership, it may face pressure from the international community to take a more active role in supporting international justice. Engaging with the ICC could serve as a demonstration of China's commitment to upholding global norms and contributing to a rules-based international order.

Another potential factor is the evolution of the ICC itself. Reforms to the ICC's procedures, governance, and mandate could address some of China's concerns about sovereignty and political bias. If the ICC becomes more inclusive and responsive to the concerns of non-member states, China may find it more palatable to engage with the court. This engagement could take the form of cooperation on specific cases or gradual steps towards ratification of the Rome Statute.

Overall, the prospects for China's future engagement with the ICC depend on a complex interplay of domestic, international, and institutional factors. While significant obstacles remain, there are potential pathways for China to take a more active role in supporting international criminal justice. Such a development would have far-reaching implications for global governance and the future of international criminal justice. Greater Chinese involvement could enhance the legitimacy and effectiveness of the ICC, encouraging other major powers to follow suit. Additionally, it would signal a commitment to upholding international legal standards, reinforcing the global rule of law.

10

Chapter 10: Comparative Perspectives

China is not the only major power with a complicated relationship with the ICC. This chapter provides a comparative analysis of China's stance on the ICC with those of other major powers, such as the United States and Russia. By examining the similarities and differences in their approaches, we can gain a deeper understanding of the geopolitical dynamics at play.

The United States, like China, has not ratified the Rome Statute, citing concerns about sovereignty and the potential for politically motivated prosecutions. The U.S. government has been particularly wary of the ICC's jurisdiction over its military personnel and officials. Despite these concerns, the United States has cooperated with the ICC on certain cases, demonstrating a pragmatic approach similar to China's.

Russia's relationship with the ICC has also been marked by tension and skepticism. Russia signed the Rome Statute but later withdrew its signature, citing concerns about the court's impartiality and effectiveness. Like China, Russia emphasizes the importance of state sovereignty and non-interference in domestic affairs. However, Russia has also faced ICC scrutiny for its actions in conflicts such as Ukraine and Syria, leading to further strain in its relationship with the court.

The comparative analysis reveals that concerns about sovereignty, political misuse, and compatibility with domestic legal systems are common among major powers. These concerns reflect broader debates about the role of international institutions in a multipolar world. While the ICC's mandate to uphold justice is universally acknowledged, the path to achieving this goal remains contested and complex.

Despite these challenges, there are also opportunities for major powers to collaborate on areas of common interest within the framework of the ICC. Issues such as counter-terrorism, human trafficking, and transnational crime require international cooperation and coordination. By finding common ground on these issues, major powers can contribute to the development of a more effective and inclusive system of international criminal justice.

11

Chapter 11: Scholarly Perspectives

To provide a well-rounded understanding of China's relationship with the ICC, this chapter presents perspectives from legal scholars and experts. These analyses and opinions offer valuable insights into the legal, political, and cultural factors influencing China's stance on the ICC. The chapter also highlights scholarly debates on the future of international criminal justice.

Legal scholars emphasize the importance of understanding China's unique legal traditions and political context when analyzing its stance on the ICC. China's blend of civil law and socialist legal principles differs significantly from the common law systems prevalent in many ICC member states. This divergence necessitates a nuanced approach to assessing China's concerns about the compatibility of legal standards and procedures.

Some experts argue that China's cautious approach to the ICC is rooted in a broader skepticism of Western-led international institutions. They contend that China's experiences with colonialism and foreign intervention have shaped its emphasis on sovereignty and non-interference. These historical and cultural factors play a crucial role in shaping China's legal diplomacy and its engagement with international justice.

Other scholars highlight the potential for constructive engagement between China and the ICC. They point to areas of common interest, such as combating transnational crime and promoting human rights, as opportunities for collaboration. By focusing on these shared goals, China and the ICC can build trust and work towards a more inclusive and effective system of international criminal justice.

The chapter also explores the potential impact of reforms to the ICC on China's engagement. Scholars suggest that addressing concerns about political bias, enhancing procedural fairness, and increasing inclusivity could make the ICC more appealing to non-member states, including China. These reforms would require a concerted effort by the international community to create a more balanced and equitable system of justice.

In conclusion, scholarly perspectives provide valuable insights into the complexities of China's relationship with the ICC. By understanding the legal, political, and cultural factors at play, we can gain a deeper appreciation of the challenges and opportunities for international criminal justice.

12

Chapter 12: Conclusion and Reflection

The final chapter offers a summary of the key points discussed throughout the book. It reflects on the significance of China's legal frontier in the context of the ICC and international justice. As China's global influence continues to grow, its approach to international criminal justice will have far-reaching implications for global governance and the rule of law.

China's relationship with the ICC is shaped by a complex interplay of domestic, international, and institutional factors. The country's emphasis on sovereignty, concerns about political misuse, and unique legal traditions all contribute to its cautious stance. However, China's active engagement in international legal forums and its strategic diplomatic maneuvering demonstrate a commitment to shaping global legal norms.

The prospects for China's future engagement with the ICC remain uncertain, but there are potential pathways for cooperation and collaboration. By addressing mutual concerns and finding common ground on issues of shared interest, China and the ICC can work towards a more effective and inclusive system of international criminal justice.

The comparative analysis with other major powers reveals common challenges and opportunities in the pursuit of global justice. The experiences of the United States and Russia highlight the broader geopolitical dynamics at play and underscore the need for a balanced and equitable approach to international criminal justice.

Scholarly perspectives provide valuable insights into the legal, political, and cultural factors influencing China's stance on the ICC. By understanding these factors, we can better appreciate the complexities of China's legal frontier and the potential for constructive engagement with the court.

In reflecting on the rise of China as a global superpower and its relationship with the ICC, this book underscores the importance of dialogue, cooperation, and mutual understanding. As the international community navigates the challenges of upholding justice in a multipolar world, China's role will be crucial in shaping the future of global governance and the rule of law.

Book Description

In *China's Legal Frontier: The Rise of a Superpower in the ICC*, we embark on a captivating exploration of China's complex relationship with the International Criminal Court (ICC). Through twelve insightful chapters, the book delves into the historical, legal, and political dimensions of this relationship, shedding light on China's evolving stance toward international criminal justice.

The journey begins with an overview of the ICC's origins and mission, setting the stage for understanding the significance of the court in the global legal landscape. As we delve deeper, we uncover China's cautious approach to international law, shaped by its emphasis on state sovereignty and non-interference in domestic affairs.

We explore the reasons behind China's decision not to ratify the Rome Statute, examining the domestic and international factors that influenced this choice. The book highlights the sovereignty dilemma, analyzing China's legal and political arguments against the ICC's potential interventions in domestic matters.

Through diplomatic maneuvering and strategic engagement, China has actively influenced international legal norms while protecting its national interests. We examine China's role in the United Nations, regional organizations, and initiatives like the Belt and Road, showcasing its growing influence in global governance.

The human rights debate takes center stage as we navigate the complexities

CHAPTER 12: CONCLUSION AND REFLECTION

of China's human rights record and its interactions with the ICC. The book also delves into the legal dimensions of the Belt and Road Initiative, exploring how China's global projects intersect with international criminal justice.

Looking ahead, the book contemplates the prospects for China's future engagement with the ICC. It provides a comparative analysis with other major powers, offering a broader perspective on the geopolitical dynamics at play.

Scholarly perspectives enrich the narrative, offering nuanced insights into the legal, political, and cultural factors shaping China's stance. The conclusion reflects on the implications of China's rise as a global superpower and its impact on the future of international criminal justice.

China's Legal Frontier: The Rise of a Superpower in the ICC is a thought-provoking journey into the intersection of law, politics, and global governance, offering readers a deeper understanding of China's evolving role in the international legal order.

www.ingramcontent.com/pod-product-compliance
Lightning Source LLC
LaVergne TN
LVHW010445070526
838199LV00066B/6201